AWS Step Functions
Retrying Failed Steps

Table of Contents

Chapter 1. Introduction

In this detailed Special Report, we delve into the intricate world of AWS Step Functions, particularly focusing on the course of action when confronting failed steps and the crucial aspect of retrying them. While it may sound like an immensely technical topic - and indeed it is - we are committed to presenting it in a conservative, straightforward manner that removes the cloak of complexity. You will find that this report isn't just a dense technical read but rather an eye-opening journey, revealing how to efficiently handle and resolve any hitches with AWS Step Functions. Whether you're a seasoned AWS user or just setting foot on this path, this Special Report has been crafted with the aim of empowering you to achieve smoother, more reliable workflows.

Chapter 2. Introduction to AWS Step Functions

Amazon Web Services (AWS) is a vast and resourceful platform that enables businesses to build and manage applications and services using a series of tools and technologies. One of these tools is AWS Step Functions, which can orchestrate distributed applications and microservices using visual workflows.

AWS Step Functions allows developers to design and execute workflows that stitch together services like AWS Lambda and Amazon ECS into feature-rich applications. Step Functions is based on state machines, and each step in the workflow is a state. This model is extremely flexible and can be adapted to many different use cases. It permits automatic error handling, parallel processing, and conditional branching of your workflows.

AWS Step Functions provides multiple advantages such as:

- Highly Scalable - Step Functions handles scaling, patching, and infrastructure management automatically, thereby providing high availability and fault tolerance for your applications.

- Full Control over Execution - Step Functions provides a console that makes it easy to inspect and debug your execution state visually.

- Extendable - Step Functions integrates with AWS services like AWS Lambda, Amazon SNS, and Amazon DynamoDB, allowing users to tap into a rich ecosystem of application development services.

2.1. The Building Blocks of AWS Step Functions

The primary building blocks of AWS Step Functions are `state machines`, `states`, and `tasks`.

- State Machine: A state machine acts as a blueprint for your entire operation or workflow. It defines the series of steps or states which will be carried out throughout the process.

- State: A state within Step Functions is a particular stage of the workflow. It could either be a task state, a choice state, a wait state, a succeed or fail state, or even a parallel state. The state dictates what happens in that specific part of the workflow.

- Tasks: Tasks are a type of state where some form of computation or work is done. They often represent a single piece of the entire operation like calling another AWS service or waiting for a manual activity to be done.

2.2. Designing and Executing Workflows with AWS Step Functions

Workflows in AWS Step Functions are defined using JSON-based Amazon States Language (ASL). ASL uses a declarative syntax to define states, inputs, outputs, and data flow in a State Machine. By using ASL, you precisely control the workflow behavior, ensure that every possible pathway and outcome is catered for, and feed output from one step as an input to the next with precise control over its format.

Execution in AWS Step Functions represents a single, fully encapsulated run of a state machine. Once a state machine is instantiated, the execution begins with the Start State and continues until an End State is reached, either Fail or Success. At any time, one can check the state of the execution, view its history, and understand the path taken.

2.3. Error Handling in AWS Step Functions

One of the essential aspects of any workflow automation tool is handling failures and errors efficiently. In AWS Step Functions, the error handling model follows a hierarchical structure where error handling is defined at a task level, then at a state machine level, and finally at an execution level.

Each Task state provides options to catch and handle various error conditions. This can range from built-in service and internal AWS issues to issues defined within the tasks of your state machine. AWS Step Functions define error fields such as "ErrorEquals", "Next", and "Retry" to handle the various conditions and determine the next step after an error has been encountered.

The service also provides features to manage retries and timeouts which allows you to configure how many times a task should be retried before being classified as a failure, and the interval between the retries. This, in conjunction with the error handling method, ensures that your workflows respond appropriately to issues and maximize their resilience.

2.4. AWS Step Functions Use Cases

Common use cases for AWS Step Functions include data transformation, IT automation, incident response, and approval workflows. For example, in data transformation workflows, AWS Step Functions can be used to cleanse, validate, transform, and move data between different data stores. In an IT automation scenario, AWS Step Functions can manage infrastructure deployment, respond to monitoring alerts, and handle incident management workflows.

The versatility of AWS Step Functions, coupled with tight integration into the AWS ecosystem, makes it an indispensable tool for building reliable, robust, and scalable workflows with improved recovery mechanisms. This comprehensive report will delve deeper into the intricacies of adapting AWS Step Functions error handling, ensuring that your workflows are resilient and reliable.

Chapter 3. Understanding the Cause of Failed Steps

Understanding the root cause of failed steps within AWS Step Functions requires a deep dive into its functions while keeping a keen eye on possible avenues where things could go astray. This process is essential as Step Functions allow you to build resilient applications by automating the coordination of tasks for multi-step workflows.

AWS Step Functions are a serverless workflow service that coordinate microservices using visual workflows. They enable you to build and update apps quickly, combine services easily, scale instantly and deal with failed executions instinctively. The AWS service provides a robust set of tools and the ability to handle error conditions, something we will be discussing comprehensively.

3.1. Step Function Execution

Step Functions work on the state machines that take a series of steps to accomplish a task. AWS enables you to design the workflows visually, breaking down the decision points, parallel tasks, timeouts, and retries. These elements are combined into the definition of a state machine.

A state machine can contain multiple types of states, including Task, Choice, Wait, Parallel, Succeed, and Fail. The execution in AWS Step Functions is composed of states, and these states comprise the information of the executed steps and their corresponding results.

A state is considered failed when the AWS Step Function can't successfully execute that state to produce outputs and continue to the next state. Whether it's an error in invoking task functions, invalid parameters or exceeding retry limits, numerous reasons can lead to failure. It is essential to understand these reasons to mitigate them in future operations.

3.2. Errors in AWS Step Functions

Errors in AWS functions can have several origins. They may be thrown by the state machine itself, by activities or service integrations, by error equalizers within a Retry or Catch field, or when an execution logically enters a Fail state.

An AWS Step Functions execution can fail due to either a system error or an error in the state machine or underlying Lambda function. The System errors such as `States.Timeout`, `States.ALL` are inherent to the AWS Step Functions engine and might occur during the execution of a task state.

Task or activity errors such as `Lambda.Unknown`, `Lambda.ServiceException`, `Lambda.AWSLambdaException`, `States.TaskFailed` occur when the task execution fails due to an issue with the task itself or its return type. The other errors are not thrown by a service, but they might experience equally.

Whenever an error is thrown in AWS Step Functions, the AWS service attempts to match the error with a list of Error Names provided in the `Catch` fields of the state.

3.3. Specific Error Cases

Let's focus on how some specific errors occur and what they signify.

1. An `InvalidParameter` error is reported when the input data required by the function is either missing or invalid. Always ensure that essential inputs are supplied and in the correct format.

2. `Lambda.AWSLambdaException` indicates that there was an issue

within the underlying Lambda function itself. This is something inherent to the function and could be due to various reasons such as invalid runtime parameters, insufficient memory, or incorrect handling of exceptions.

3. Task failure errors such as `Lambda.ServiceException` or `States.TaskFailed` could occur when an error is encountered while executing a task or activity. This could be due to an error returned by an upstream API, exception thrown by code within the service, or exceeding service limits.

4. Catch and rerun failed executions with a structured process. These errors can be captured in the `Catch` field, and the workflow can be designed to rerun failed executions.

3.4. Identifying Failed Steps

The AWS Step Functions' execution event history can help identify the failed steps. The visual workflow in AWS Management Console also provides visual cues as to which step in the process failed. Failed states will be signified in the red, and green signifies successful states.

A step function's state can be evaluated by the output from the Lambdas they trigger or the function itself. You could inspect the `Input` and `Output` JSON of individual steps.

For Lambda task states, you could examine the logs in the CloudWatch. You can follow the AWS Step Functions execution event history to track paths that were taken through the state machine.

3.5. Understanding and Reacting to Timeout Errors

When a state machine is executing and its state runs longer than the `TimeoutSeconds` value, a `States.Timeout` error is thrown.

In AWS Step Functions, the timeout error is quite common and can be addressed by increasing the timeout value or by designing the state machine in such a manner that it copes with the runtime conditions.

It's crucial to conduct an error analysis after encountering a failure. This process will not only help you resolve the existing issue but also prevent similar errors in the future. Understanding the root cause of these failures and making defensive coding a core part of your application design will ensure efficient and smoother operations.

Thus, understanding and handling errors in AWS Step Functions is more than just firefighting; it is an important aspect of designing resilient, fault-tolerant applications that handle operations with grace and efficiency.

Chapter 4. Basic Concepts of Retry Policies

To understand how retrying works in AWS Step Functions, it's essential to start with some basic concepts that underpin retry policies. Let's start this journey by understanding the fundamental elements - Error Handling, and Retry and Catch Fields.

4.1. Error Handling

In AWS Step Functions, tasks are the functional components in a state machine that represent sections of the workflow implementation. Tasks execute specific units of work by calling other AWS services, including Lambda or DynamoDB. A task either succeeds or fails, and based on its outcome, different paths are followed in the state machine execution.

Errors can occur during a state machine execution for many reasons - maybe a service a task is calling is temporarily unavailable, a function has an unhandled exception or a wrong input parameter is provided. AWS Step Functions leverages errors to change the execution flow in the state machine.

When a task encounters an error, these can be of two types:

1. System errors: These are AWSError types generated by AWS Step Functions infrastructure layer. Examples include "States.Timeout" or "States.TaskFailed".

2. Service errors: These are errors thrown by AWS services that the task is communicating with. Example: a Lambda function throwing an error.

The errors thrown by tasks can be caught and handled, leading us to the next set of concepts - Retry and Catch Fields.

4.2. Retry and Catch Fields

A task in an AWS State machine can have two important fields in its state definition, that handle task failure: Retry and Catch.

The Retry field defines a policy to handle failures in the tasks (service or system errors). When a task fails, the retry policy attempts to execute the task again, up to a user-defined maximum number of attempts.

The Catch field allows the state machine to continue execution at another state when an error is thrown.

It's important to note that retries (if defined) happen before catch fields are evaluated. This means the state machine will try to accomplish the task as specified in the retry policy first, and, if all attempts fail, it will then evaluate the catch field and proceed.

4.3. Retry Fields

There are five important parameters when defining a retry policy:

1. `ErrorEquals` - The list of error names that the retry policy will match with. When matching error names, the policy matches exact error names but allows for wildcard entries as well wherein '*' would match all errors.

2. `IntervalSeconds` - The time interval (in seconds) between two consecutive retry attempts. The default is one second.

3. `MaxAttempts`- The maximum number of retry attempts. If this value is 0, the task doesn't retry.

4. `BackoffRate` - The rate at which the retry interval increases with each attempt. This uses the exponential backoff algorithm. The default value is 2.0.

5. `MaxIntervalSeconds` - Defines the maximum interval between two

retry attempts. This is not supported for all AWS services.

Here is an example of a retry policy for reference:

```
"Retry": [
  {
    "ErrorEquals": [ "Lambda.ServiceException",
"Lambda.AWSLambdaException",
"Lambda.SdkClientException"],
    "IntervalSeconds": 2,
    "MaxAttempts": 6,
    "BackoffRate": 2.0
  }
]
```

These fields when configured properly, could allow a workflow to handle intermediate failures seamlessly, retrying whenever possible and ensuring progression even when things go wrong.

4.4. Catch Fields

Catch fields come into play after all retry attempts fail (or if no retry policy is defined). They intercept uncaught exceptions and allow the state machine to continue its execution at specified states.

These work very similarly to 'Catch' blocks in programming languages, and also allow the matching of specific or all errors.

The syntax is similar to Retry fields, as shown below:

```
"Catch": [
  {
    "ErrorEquals": ["States.ALL"],
    "Next": "RecoveryState"
```

```
    }
  ]
```

In the example, if an error (any error - "States.ALL"), arises that is not handled within the scope of the task's retries, the execution will continue from the state termed "RecoveryState".

When using Catch fields, it's recommended to include catch-all error handling at the end of a Catch block to ensure none of the unanticipated errors cause a state machine failure.

In conclusion, AWS Step Functions provides powerful error handling and retry mechanisms to build robust workflows. To achieve smoother, more reliable workflows, it's crucial to use these Retry and Catch fields effectively. By understanding how these work and by doing proper planning, it's possible to create solid fault-tolerant applications on AWS. We hope this introduction to retry policies sets you on the right path to explore more complex state machine designs and workflows.

Chapter 5. Designing Effective Retry Strategies

AWS Step Functions, incidentally designed to regulate sequential and parallel tasks for varying applications, may not always function with unfailing precision. Instances of failure are, after all, common in any complex software ecosystem and Step Functions is no different.

Let's explore the scenario where a step within the function does not execute as expected. Rather than having the entire process come undone when this occurs, we can incorporate a retry and error handling strategy. By doing so, we can also ensure the efficient and seamless operation of our workflows. This exploration demands care and detail. But fret not, the subject can be simplified by partitioning it into manageable segments - five sub-chapters, to be precise.

5.1. Understanding the Need for Retry Strategies

Failure is a ubiquity within the realm of software; acknowledging this fact and anticipating errors is a necessary measure in building robust applications. AWS Step Functions, like any other software system, is not immune to failures. The objective thus lies in establishing effective defense strategies against these inevitable disruptions, one of which is using a retry mechanism.

An unrestrained approach to handling a failed step could plunge the whole system into chaos, rerunning steps indiscriminately and consuming valuable resources. Empowering your Step Functions with a judicious retry strategy not only preserves resources but also substantively improves the chances of successful step execution.

Think of a retry strategy as an insurance policy for your workflow, a failsafe that ensures your step functions continue endeavoring to perform their task in the event of a failure. AWS thankfully provides `Retry`, a state that can be effectively leveraged to build intricate and beneficial retry strategies.

5.2. The Mechanics of Retry in AWS Step Functions

Before we dive headfirst into the design of the retry strategies, it's essential to understand what a `Retry` is in AWS Step Functions.

In essence, `Retry` is a field within the state machine structure that lays out conditions for retrying failed error states. It comprises three main attributes:

- `ErrorEquals`: This attribute represents an array containing strings of the errors for which to initiate the retry policy.

- `IntervalSeconds`: The minimal waiting period between retry attempts.

- `BackoffRate`: A heft multiplier that extends the delay period between each consecutive retry attempt. It essentially uses the concept of exponential backoff to progressively increase the waiting time, thereby avoiding rapid, continuous retry attempts.

- `MaxAttempts`: This captures the maximum number of attempts at executing a state before declaring it as 'Fail.'

Effectively handling these four parameters can construct a powerful and robust retry mechanism.

5.3. Implementing a Basic Retry Strategy

Getting started with a retry strategy necessitates dealing with occasional failures rather than hiccups at each step. For the first measure of defense against sporadic failures, a `DefaultRetry` strategy can be applied, fortified with sensible values. An example setup of a `DefaultRetry` could look like this in JSON:

```
"Retry": [{
    "ErrorEquals": ["States.ALL"],
    "IntervalSeconds": 5,
    "MaxAttempts": 5,
    "BackoffRate": 2.0
}]
```

In the given example, errors of all types will initiate the retry policy. There will be a minimum wait of five seconds between each retry attempt, with the waiting period doubling each time due to the backoff rate. This retry mechanism will cap off at five attempts.

5.4. Advancing Towards More Sophisticated Retry Strategies

After perfecting the basics, it's time to employ more advanced safeguarding tactics. In the theatre of complex AWS systems, a one-size-fits-all approach may not suffice due to an array of error types and frequencies of failures that can suddenly emerge.

One such method involves setting up multiple conditional retry blocks. Each block would target a specific category of error, and thus, be calibrated with a unique retry strategy catering to the error's characteristics.

For instance, network-related issues often require more time for recovery, so they could benefit from a more extended wait period or even a larger number of attempts. On the flip side, a runtime error due to software bug may not be rectified by mere retries, making a rapid failure desirable.

Another advanced strategy is designing custom backoff logic that modulates the retry intervals more finely according to your specific needs. This could involve using AWS Lambda functions or external libraries offering custom backoff algorithms.

All in all, the secret to designing efficient retry strategies lies in understanding the nature of the failures faced and tailoring the strategy accordingly.

5.5. Important Considerations for Implementing Retry Strategies

In concluding this chapter, we can't overlook some critical considerations. Deciding when to use a specific retry strategy requires knowledge of one's own system and the capabilities that AWS provides.

There is a fine line between being aggressive and conservative when deciding retry strategies. An aggressive strategy could overburden the system by rapidly rerunning failed states, while an overly-conservative strategy might lead to delays due to extended periods between retries.

One should also consider the implications of using a `Catch` field. If used carelessly, a `Catch` can effectively suppress failures, causing errors to go unnoticed.

Finally, while AWS Step Functions allows us to build complex retry strategies, it's crucial to strike balance by ensuring your strategies are manageable, maintainable, and effective. Unnecessarily convoluted strategies may create challenges for monitoring, debugging, and system improvement.

Mastering the design of effective retry strategies can not only help save costs but also enormously improve the reliability and resilience of your AWS Step Functions. Hence, thoughtful planning and systematic implementation are instrumental for building successful error handling methods in your Step Functions.

Chapter 6. Implementing Retry Policies in AWS Step Functions

Understanding functions that fail and their repair is an integral part of Step Functions. For purposes of this discussion, we will focus on the mechanism, referred to as "Retry Policies," that allows us to address these failures systematically. Here's a comprehensive guide to implementing Retry Policies in AWS Step Functions.

6.1. Establishing the Need for Retry Policies

Developers often confront the condition where certain functions may fail during their execution. These conditions usually are not under our control, as they may depend upon external dependencies that potentially fail. These dependencies include network latency, unavailability of third-party services, or transient issues. It is indeed crucial to handle these uncertain conditions gracefully to ensure the smooth execution of workflows. Here's where AWS Step Functions' Retry Policies provide an essential safety net.

A Retry Policy in AWS Step Functions allows you to automatically retry a failed task or state without having to define this logic within the function itself. It provides a reliable way to deal with transient issues, making your serverless workflows more resilient.

6.2. Configuring Retry Policies

To configure Retry Policies, you need to provide Retry blocks in your AWS Step Function's state. Each block contains three distinct fields: .

ErrorEquals:Defines the list of Error names that the state can encounter for which the AWS Step Function can attempt a Retry. . IntervalSeconds:Defines the waiting time between retries. . MaxAttempts:Defines the maximum attempts of retries.

You may provide multiple retry blocks, and AWS will prioritize them in the order they're stated. This means AWS will evaluate the first retry block. If the error falls into this category, it will retry according to the rules specified in this block. If not, it will proceed to the second block and so on.

For instance, your state machine definition in AWS Step Functions with a Retry block may look like follows:

```
"HelloWorld": {
    "Type": "Task",
    "Resource": "arn:aws:lambda:us-east-
1:123456789012:function:HelloWorld",
    "Retry": [
        {
            "ErrorEquals": ["CustomError"],
            "IntervalSeconds": 1,
            "MaxAttempts": 2
        }
    ],
    "End": true
}
```

In the above example, if a function fails with a CustomError, AWS Step Functions will wait for 1 second before retrying the function. It will retry this function twice.

6.3. Using Wildcards in Retry Policies

There's a wildcard operator, represented by `"States.ALL"`. If you're not sure about the kind of errors your task state might face or you wish to be resilient against unplanned errors, this comes in quite handy.

Here's how you can use it:

```
"Retry": [
  {
      "ErrorEquals": ["States.ALL"],
      "IntervalSeconds": 5,
      "MaxAttempts": 5
  }
]
```

In this case, irrespective of the error type that caused the function to fail, AWS Step Functions will retry the function after waiting for 5 seconds. It will attempt to retry five times in total.

6.4. Implementing Backoff Logic

It is crucial to wisely set the wait time between retries and the maximum number of retries, else you might exhaust all your retries very quickly. For improving the efficiency of retries, AWS Step Functions offer exponential backoff logic with jitter.

The backoff logic is represented with two additional parameters: . `BackoffRate`: Each consecutive retry attempt will wait twice as long as the previous. . `MaxBackoffSeconds`: It sets a maximum limit for the waiting time between retry attempts.

An example of implementing backoff logic would be:

```
"Retry": [
    {
        "ErrorEquals": ["CustomError"],
        "IntervalSeconds": 2,
        "MaxAttempts": 5,
        "BackoffRate": 2.0,
        "MaxBackoffSeconds": 60
    }
]
```

6.5. Catching Failures

In case your retries have not been successful, Step Functions allow you to catch these failures and respond accordingly. A "Catch" block can be defined to catch specific errors and direct the state machine towards an appropriate state.

An example of Catch block usage:

```
"Catch": [
    {
        "ErrorEquals": ["States.ALL"],
        "Next": "CatchAllFallback"
    }
]
```

In this example, it will catch any error and direct the state machine towards "CatchAllFallback" state.

Ultimately, implementing Retry Policies in AWS Step Functions isn't about staving off failure entirely—it's about handling those failures in a way that makes your workflows robust, reliable, and resilient. With a carefully crafted retry policy, you can reduce the impact of failing states and ensure that your serverless workflows operate smoothly, even when the unforeseen happens.

Chapter 7. Case Study: Resolving Real-World Failed Steps

In the heart of AWS Step Functions, we encounter various real-world scenarios where steps may often fail, disrupting the smooth terrain of our operations. In this section, we unlock multiple experiences that discuss failed steps, showcase how to determine the source of the failure, and uncover successful strategies to retry them efficiently.

7.1. Breakdown of a Real-World Scenario

We begin with a realistic scenario: executing an AWS Step Function to orchestrate a series of tasks designed around data processing. The steps include:

1. Extract valuable data from an Amazon S3 bucket,

2. Transform the extracted data with AWS Lambda,

3. Load the transformed data into an Amazon Redshift cluster,

4. Finally, send a notification with Amazon SNS upon successful completion.

Suppose the third step fails. The Lambda function simply didn't manage to load the data into the Redshift cluster. This failure prompts AWS Step Functions to throw an error.

7.2. Analyzing the Failure

First, we must understand the nature of the failure. The AWS Step Functions console maintains logs of each task, assisting in tracing the failure source back to its roots. Let's see two main categories of failures:

1. Transient Failures: These are temporary, sporadic issues that may resolve momentarily. Diagnosing these errors can include checking if the service hosting the task (Lambda, in our example) is experiencing any known issues, or if network latency is causing a timeout.

2. Systematic Failures: These point towards a more systematic malfunction such as programming errors, incorrect expressions in the state machine definition, or incorrect IAM permissions.

Market data feeds often include upper and lower limit price bands. If the limit bands are incorrect for any security, it is a systematic error, needing correction before re-initiating the feed process.

7.3. Implementing Retry Logic

After diagnosing the nature of the failure, we can refine our step tasks with a retry strategy. Retry strategies in AWS Step Functions include two key components: `MaxAttempts` and `BackoffRate`.

1. MaxAttempts specifies the maximum number of times the service should retry the execution of a task after it fails.

2. BackoffRate determines the rate at which AWS should increase the waiting period between retries.

As a best practice, avoid setting MaxAttempts too high, especially if the failures are systematic; this will only increase the time until the state machine execution reaches its terminal state.

7.4. Handling Failures in Step Functions

Next, what do we do if retrying the failed step doesn't succeed? AWS Step Functions provides two means of handling these situations: Catchers and Fail States.

1. Catchers are designed to catch an error and route the state machine execution to a different state.

2. Fail States stop the state machine execution and mark it as a failure.

7.5. Resolving the Scenario

Now, getting back to our scenario. The Redshift Load operation fails due to transient network issues. You could add retry logic to this step task where MaxAttempts=3 and BackoffRate=2. This allows the operation to retry three times before failing, with increasing delay.

But let's say the issue persists, and all retry attempts fail. In this case, add a Catcher that routes execution to a different state where you could use SNS to notify the administrators about the failure. They can then manually resolve the issue and resume the process.

7.6. Lessons Learned and Best Practices

Working through this scenario offers us two valuable insights: thoroughness in error-logging strategy and the sagacity of the recovery process.

Remember, thorough logs provide the deepest insight into what could be causing a failure. They also help to separate transient failures from systematic ones, and help you choose the correct recovery path.

AWS Step Functions are powerful but require careful strategy. Implementing retries, catchers, and fail states properly can improve your application's resilience significantly. Be sure to use the feature suite wisely and optimize for better results.

Closing thoughts: The ability to detect, diagnose, and handle failures robustly, has a direct impact on how efficiently a system can bounce back from issues, ensuring scalability, resilience, and trust in your AWS solutions.

Chapter 8. AWS Step Functions Error Handling Techniques

Failure is part and parcel of any computing process, and AWS Step Functions are no exception. Identifying and resolving these failures can significantly enhance workflow reliability. In this detailed discourse, we will be looking into the various techniques, strategies, and best practices for handling errors in AWS Step Functions.

8.1. Catching and Retrying Failures

Failures in AWS Step Functions are inevitable, but knowing how to catch and retry them can significantly reduce their impact. If an AWS Lambda function used in a state machine throws an error, the execution fails unless the error is caught.

AWS Step Functions provide Retry and Catch fields at the state level that offer fine-grained control over error handling. If neither Catch nor Retry fields are provided, the execution fails immediately. Let's look at these in further detail.

1. **Retry Field**:

The Retry field allows AWS Step Functions to automatically retry the execution of a failed state. For instance, network issues or temporary unavailability of a service can cause a state to fail. However, if these issues are resolved quickly, simply retrying the state execution might solve the problem.

Here's a simple example in asciidoc syntax:

```
"Retry": [
```

```
    {
        "ErrorEquals": ["States.ALL"],
        "IntervalSeconds": 5,
        "MaxAttempts": 5,
        "BackoffRate": 2.0
    }
]
```

This specifies that if any error occurs (specified by "States.ALL"), the state should be retried after an interval of 5 seconds. The failure can be retried a maximum of 5 times, with each retry interval increasing by a factor of 2 (known as Exponential Backoff).

1. **Catch Field**:

The Catch field is used to catch errors in a state and divert the execution flow to a different state. Here is an asciidoc example:

```
"Catch": [
    {
        "ErrorEquals": ["States.ALL"],
        "Next": "RecoveryState"
    }
]
```

This configuration diverts the execution flow to the RecoveryState if any error occurs.

8.2. Error Types in AWS Step Functions

AWS provides several built-in error types. These include:

- States.ALL: Matches any error that occurs during the state's execution.

- States.Timeout: Matches when the state's execution exceeds the state's Max Duration.

- Lambda.ServiceException: Matches when any error occurs within the AWS Lambda service.

- And others.

You can also define custom error names in your Lambda functions and create specialized catch blocks or retry policies for them.

```
"ErrorEquals": ["CustomError"]
```

This becomes very handy when you want different states to handle different types of errors differently.

8.3. The Right Balance between Retries and Catches

While retries and catches can address the issue of failures, they can lengthen the execution time if not appropriately designed. If the cause of the failure does not fall under transient errors or isn't something that can be resolved with a simple retry, a retry configuration can lead the state machine into a loop of retries/catches without any satisfactory fix.

Similarly, catch blocks, while enabling us to handle errors gracefully, can lead to a complex state machine due to many diverting paths from different states. The best practice is to juxtapose retries and catches intelligently, considering the nature and causes of possible errors. Backoff rates and maximum attempts should be configured judiciously for retries.

8.4. Using Heartbeat Configuration

AWS Step Functions provides the HeartbeatSeconds parameter, a feature that helps in handling hung states. If the task does not send heartbeat pulses or complete within the specified time, AWS Step Functions treats the task as failed.

```
"HeartbeatSeconds": 300
```

This code configures a timeout of 300 seconds for the heartbeat of a task.

8.5. Logging Failures for Diagnostics

In addition to catching and retrying, AWS Step Functions also provide the capability to log the error information for further diagnostics. Using Amazon CloudWatch Logs with your state machine is instrumental in achieving this.

To sum up, error handling in AWS Step Functions involves a careful and deliberate arrangement of catch and retry configurations, judicious use of heartbeat timeouts, and effective diagnostics via logging. Correct error handling strategies bolster the reliability and robustness of the AWS Step Functions workflows, paving the way to cohesive, sustainable, and effective serverless applications.

Chapter 9. Optimizing Workflows with Robust Retry Mechanisms

Efficient application development demands the ability to manage and mitigate failures. In the context of AWS Step Functions, it's crucial to design and implement robust retry mechanisms that enhance your workflow's resilience. This chapter will equip you with a profound understanding of these mechanisms, demystifying how they work, and presenting proven strategies to harness their potential.

9.1. Understanding Step Function Failures

AWS Step Functions coordinate individual services into serverless workflows that you can create and modify visually. When a step in a workflow encounters a runtime error, Step Functions consider the step as a 'Failure.' This could include exceptions thrown by task states, timeouts, or when particular conditions are not met. It is important to note that failed steps don't necessarily mean that your overall workflow fails. However, they can lead to workflow interruptions or inefficient processing if not handled properly.

9.2. The Mechanics of Retry and Catch

Retrying failed steps can immensely improve the robustness of your workflows. AWS Step Functions provide the 'Retry' and 'Catch' error handling features to manage such scenarios.

Retry waits for a specific interval before re-executing the failed step, while Catch takes an alternative course of action when a step fails. A well-defined Retry policy coupled with Catch error handlers can ensure that your workflows continue to function smoothly even when individual tasks fail.

9.3. Configuring a Retry Policy

You can configure a Retry policy for any state that can encounter a runtime error. The fields you define in a Retry policy include 'ErrorEquals,' 'IntervalSeconds,' 'MaxAttempts,' and 'BackoffRate.'

'ErrorEquals' is an array where you specify the error types to retry. 'IntervalSeconds' is the waiting period before the first retry attempt, and 'MaxAttempts' is the number of retry attempts. 'BackoffRate' is a multiplier that increases the waiting period for subsequent retry attempts.

It's crucial to choose sensible values for these fields aligned with your use case. For example, an immediate retry wouldn't make sense when dealing with network-related issues, as they often require some time to resolve.

9.4. Utilizing Catch Error Handling

On the other hand, 'Catch' error handlers allow you to define a state to execute if an error is caught. You can specify different Catch branches for different error types, enabling your workflows to adapt to various failure scenarios.

The branch that is followed when an error is caught has access to the error information including the Error Name, Error Cause, and Error Message. This can be used for debugging or to decide the next course of action.

9.5. Combining Retry and Catch for Reliable Workflows

Using Retry and Catch together can render your workflows incredibly resilient. For example, you can design your workflow with a Retry policy that gives a step three attempts before it triggers the Catch handler. The Retry mechanism ensures transient errors don't cause workflow failures, and the Catch feature ensures there's an alternate path for persistent errors.

It's vital to understand that Retry and Catch provide you with formidable tools to enhance your workflow's error handling capability. They can ensure that your orchestration doesn't immediately surrender to runtime errors, potentially saving you from unnecessary manual intervention and system downtime.

9.6. Error Handling Best Practices

When setting up Retry and Catch mechanisms, there are a few best practices you can follow. First, avoid infinite retries. They contribute to a resource drain and can delay the identification of the error source. Second, use meaningful error messages. Detailed and informative error messages assist immensely during the debugging process. Lastly, vary the Retry periods based on the nature of the failure. This variation will lead to more efficient handling of error situations.

In conclusion, it's clear that the strategic use of Retry and Catch in AWS Step Functions can significantly enhance the reliability and efficiency of your workflows. They provide a robust framework for handling potential issues, thereby augmenting your productivity as a developer and outcome reliability. As you continue to use AWS Step Functions, aspire to implement these techniques to truly optimize your workflow.

Remember, robust retry mechanisms are not a panacea for application errors; they need to be part of a broader error handling and application robustness strategy. Nonetheless, their strategic deployment will earn you greater confidence in your applications, making you more equipped to tackle the ever-evolving technological landscape.

Chapter 10. Continuous Monitoring and Improving Retry Policies

AWS Step Functions offer incredible abilities to manage and coordinate different parts of your computational resources to yield an efficient and smooth workflow. Among these aspects, retry policies have a nonpareil role in providing robust and persistent performance. As the name suggests, retry policies determine how Step Functions handle failed steps, which might result due to service exceptions, service faults, or throttling errors, making them an irreplaceable part of AWS Step Functions' error management.

As we venture into the domain of monitoring and improving retry policies, it's essential to comprehend the scope of what these mechanisms hold and how they can be designed and refactored to serve your workflow better.

10.1. Importance of Monitoring

Monitoring retry policies is as significant as implementing them. A system without supervision might repetitively encounter problems that could otherwise be avoided. Routinely monitoring your applications through AWS's built-in tools, such as AWS CloudWatch, can give insights into retry attempts and the causes of failures, enabling you to fine-tune your retry policies if they constantly fail.

```
1. __Logs__: AWS Step Functions record logs about state
transitions, including information about any retry
attempts executed.
2. __Metrics__: Metrics about the number of failed
activities, Lambda functions, and executions provide
```

quantitative data that can guide your policy
adjustments.
3. __Events__: AWS EventBridge can be set up to respond
to execution state changes, including retry attempts, to
implement customized responses.

Monitoring the three facets above will grant you visibility into your
system's behavior. Without this, optimal retry policies and
troubleshooting elusive issues would be a daunting task.

10.2. Analyzing and Understanding Failures

In tandem with monitoring, understanding why steps fail will guide
you to formulate more effective retry policies. While some failures
occur due to temporary network issues or lack of resources and can
be resolved by retrying after some delay, others might stem from
configuration problems or bugs in the application code.

1. __Transient Failures__: These are temporary issues in
the infrastructure, such as network instability or
insufficient computational resources. The Retry field in
state definitions is the appropriate place to manage
these issues.

2. __Permanent Failures__: Permanent failures are
typically the result of deeper issues in your workflow,
like incorrect state definitions or bugs in your
application code. In this case, redressal requires more
than just tweaking retry policies; it demands
rebalancing or eliminating the fault.

So, a profound understanding of what's causing your failures:

transient or permanent, is instrumental to tailor your retry policies.

10.3. Design and Refinement Retry Policies

Now that we have a grasp on why steps fail and how to monitor them, the next stage is to design retry policies and the art of iteratively improving them based on insights gathered.

1. __Defining Retry Policies__: AWS Step Functions allow you to specify a Retry field in your state definition that determines how many times the step is retried after a failure, the delay between retries, and a backoff rate that controls the rate at which the delay increases.

2. __Improving Retry Policies__: Policies can be fine-tuned based on accumulated data, modifying parameters like maximum attempts and backoff rate. For example, if a function frequently fails due to a lack of resources and only succeeds after several attempts, increasing the delay between retries or decreasing the backoff rate might solve the problem.

3. __Testing and Validation__: Continuous testing and validation of your retry policies are crucial. AWS provides tools and services, such as Load testing, AWS Fault Injection Simulator, and A/B testing, that allow you to simulate different scenarios and assess the behavior of your retry policies, providing a practical benchmark for their performance.

This iterative process of design, refinement, and validation will equip you to create resilient retry policies that improve the reliability and efficiency of your workflow.

10.4. Automating the Process

Finally, let's delve into the possibilities of automating the task of monitoring and refining retry policies. AWS offers several services that can be used for this, including AWS Lambda, AWS CloudWatch, and AWS EventBridge.

```
1. __Anomaly Detection__: AWS CloudWatch can be set up
to detect anomalies in your Step Functions metrics,
enabling you to automate your monitoring process.

2. __Lambda Functions__: AWS Lambda functions can be
written to automatically respond to anomalous events,
modify retry policies, or even alert you when the number
of retry attempts on a step exceeds a certain threshold.

3. __AWS EventBridge__: EventBridge can be configured to
respond to execution state changes and activate
remediation processes, like debugging or modifying retry
policies.
```

Automation does not eliminate the need for careful monitoring and occasional manual intervention, but it certainly reduces the workload and makes the process more reliable and efficient.

In conclusion, monitoring and iteratively improving retry policies in AWS Step Function is an imperative task that ensures the smooth functioning of your workflows. Acknowledging the causes of step failures and meticulously implementing and refining your retry policies can drastically augment your workflow's resilience and reliability. By leveraging the AWS ecosystem's powerful services, you can automate this task, making it an even more streamlined operation.

Chapter 11. Looking Ahead: The Future of AWS Step Functions Error Handling

As we sit at the precipice of unparalleled technological advancements, it is only fitting that we strive to explore what the future might hold for AWS Step Functions and error handling. The evolution of AWS Step Functions has proven the dynamic and limitless potential of the platform. Therefore, as we venture into the uncharted waters of the future, some informed assumptions and predictions can be made about the trajectory of this service and how error handling will be managed.

11.1. The Increase in Resiliency

In the foreseeable future, we may expect enhancements in the overall stability and resilience of AWS Step Functions. As the quest for staying error-free remains the holy grail of any software service, AWS could possibly focus on robust features and tools that make the service more resistant to failures. This would directly result in reduced instances of errors, which subsequently reduces the need for error handling.

Improvements in resiliency may also present themselves in the form of better recovery capabilities. Currently, AWS Step Functions provides a "Retry" facility which users can utilize to rerun failed functions. Perhaps, in the future, AWS may begin to offer more holistic recovery options. For instance, an automatic checkpointing mechanism might be introduced to save the state of active functions at regular intervals and efficiently restart from the last recorded state in the event of a failure. This would ensure minimal data loss and disruption, all the while retaining the economical benefit of not having to retry from the start.

11.2. Intensified Focus on Error Prevention

Another transformative change could be seen in the fundamental approach towards error handling. Instead of concentrating on how to manage the aftermath of errors, there might be a gradual shift towards error prevention. Amazon has already begun to show inklings of such a strategy with the provision of extensive debugging and testing tools within the AWS Step Function service like X-Ray Tracing, CloudWatch Logs, etc. These orchestrated efforts around error prevention would likely intensify over the years, potentially even going so far as utilizing machine learning algorithms to predict function failures before they occur, allowing preemptive measures to be taken.

11.3. Seamless Integration and Collaboration

There's a high possibility of closer integration of AWS Step Functions with other AWS services as well as third-party tools. This will drastically improve the overall debugging experience by providing comprehensive visibility into workflows and the related failure points. The possibility of a unified dashboard, which seamlessly brings together insights from multiple AWS services like X-Ray, Lambda, and CloudWatch could possibly be introduced. This will foster an environment of quicker and efficient debugging, allowing AWS Step Function users to nip errors in the bud, reducing the load on error handling mechanisms.

11.4. Evolution of Retry Policies and Error Fallbacks

Looking ahead, we might envisage an evolution in the governance around retry policies and error fallbacks. Currently, it's up to the user to define these properties, but with machine learning and AI becoming more integral to software services, AWS might potentially provide suggestions or even automatic configurations for these aspects. This assistance from AWS could be driven by an analysis of previous function invocations, error patterns, or even benchmarking against global best practices. Not only would this ease the burden on the users but potentially result in more effective and optimized error handling.

In conclusion, there is immense promise in the future of AWS Step Functions and error handling. While it's hard to ascertain with absolute certainty the shape of things to come, a trajectory towards advanced resilience, improved focus on error prevention, seamless integration, and evolution of retry policies seems plausible. This evolution, oriented to anticipate and preempt errors before they occur instead of merely reacting to them post-occurrence, would be pioneering in the realm of serverless computing.

AWS Step Functions and its approach to managing failures continue to evolve. As we have delved deep into the possibilities which lie ahead, it's apparent that the future holds vast potential for more efficient and effective ways to handle errors. The intrigue and promise of the future only serve to fortify the significance of staying abreast with emerging developments in this space, ready to leverage these advances at your own pace and requirement. As AWS continues on its quest for the optimal balance between performance, error management, and recovery, the future of AWS Step Functions error handling looks bright and empowering.